I Never Imagined
A *Pen* WOULD
CHANGE MY LIFE

I Never Imagined A *Pen* WOULD CHANGE MY LIFE

BARBARA JEANNE FISHER
WITH **MITCHELL HOLLAND**

Copyright © 2025 Barbara Jeanne Fisher

All rights reserved. No part of this book may be used or reproduced in any manner whatsoever without written permission of the author. Published 2025.

Printed in the United States of America.

ISBN: 978-1-63385-559-5
Library of Congress Control Number: 2025913723

Published by
Word Association Publishers
205 Fifth Avenue
Tarentum, Pennsylvania 15084

www.wordassociation.com
1.800.827.7903

Barbara's Dedication

To Mitchell Holland

Mitch, we did it! When you were not on my *People Who Inspired Me* page in the book Julie made about me, it made me think! You have been in my life for so long, and in all roles of it, you have been there for both me and my family. You were not only an advisor but even more a best friend. You wanted a book, but I do not think back then you knew that you would be writing one with me! That is wonderful.

Thank you so much, for everything. God bless you and be with you and your family. I hope we can continue being best friends forever. You did a great job on your part of the book. I always told my writing students, Write *with Your Hearts*! You made me cry, laugh, and all the other things a good author can do! Many thanks for a job well done!

Thanks, Mitch, for throwing that Pen at me! I will treasure that day forever as I will our friendship. God bless you always,

Forever and Always, Barbara Jeanne Fisher

Mitchell's Dedication

I would like to dedicate this book to God. I have always believed that He should be first in all we do. Secondly, If I did not have a religious class to learn about my Deity, I might never have had the experience to witness the design of the human mind, the hand eye coordination, and the ability for the opposition movement of our hands. With our unique design of our thumb being in a saddle joint, the movement that allows us to close in, allows for us to catch items efficiently. In this book the item was a pen tossed to a teacher by an eighth grade student!

To my lovely wife, Kathleen, who behind the scenes always believes in what I do and is always willing to help me in any possible way. Thank you so much for making our life together so special, and encouraging me as I worked on this book! My kids, I am told that when I am asked about my kids my eyes fill with love telling their stories through my experiences. *Love you kids!*

I would like to thank my parents Dick and Dianne (in 2018 passed on from this world) for without their love, I would not be in existence, especially since I am the seventh child in the family. Their dedication to their faith has been pressed onto me and I unto my children, that God is to be first and foremost, to attend church regularly and to continue in the education of life and the love that God has provided. *Thanks Mom and Dad*!

Last but not least to the church of my youth and now, Sacred Heart Parish of Fremont, OH. If that parish did not have a CCD class, I never would have had the chance to meet Barbara and Julie. Without all the people mentioned above, I would never have been the co-author of this book. It's funny how life has a way of putting people into other's lives, how they sometime fit together like a puzzle! The faith, the ability to catch by design, the ball point pen, for family and for the teachers. Thank you Barb for this opportunity to express my thoughts on paper in the career that you believe in and taught.

Part 1

February 1, 2025

Recently, my daughter decided to make a book about my entire life. It took days, even months to gather all the photos, stories from people, and new writing for the book. I was amazed as I watched her putting it all together. When it was done, the entire life story from birth to now, was between the beautiful covers was ready to print.

The completed book has been passed around. I am amazed at how many of my friends love to look at it! I enjoyed sharing it with them, and listening to the comments they made over the places I have gone with my career, my wonderful family, and one very special section included my friends who have influenced me.

Every day, I thank God for my life, my family and for sure my friends. I am writing this as I recall the beginning of a very special friendship that has lasted so many wonderful years. Mitch, this one is for you!

My Story

Many years ago, I heard that the CCD class at our Parish was in need of teachers for the upcoming class that fall. My daughter and I had the second grade class the year before. That was fun, and nice and sort of easy. But the idea of older students made both of us eager to try that.

We contacted the person in charge and were given the 8th grade. She told us, "We really need a few more teachers, I am so glad you decided to take this class! A word of warning! The last three teachers quit! They could not handle them!"

Yes! Yikes! What could a medium size group of eighth grade students do to scare adults away? My daughter and I thought about it, and then decided to accept the challenge. So begins my story about Mitch!

The students were all in their chairs when I walked in the classroom that first day. They were all talking at the same time, and I did not think it was a good idea to begin my time with them by correcting them.

I clapped my hands a few times to get their attention, then seeing that did not work, clapped them again. I stood and waited until every one of them was quiet.

I thought introducing myself and Julie first was best, then have each of them tell us who they were. Sounded easy! Right!

I started with, "My name Is Barbara Fisher, my daughter, Julie and I are going to be your teachers for this class. We look forward to spending the time with you."

Without warning a ball point pen came flying through the air at me! It missed and fell to the floor. I picked it up. I just knew whoever threw it at me was having the joke of his life, and felt proud of himself for being brave enough to greet me that way in front of his fellow students.

Holding the pen, and looking out I recognized the boy that "was so generous to loan it to me!" Calling him by name, with a smile on my face, I said, "Why thank you Mitch, how did you know I needed this? How can I ever thank you?"

All eyes were on me, and I could tell that they were surprised at my reaction. Most of them laughed because it turned out so unexpectedly! I loved it!

After that we had each student tell us his or her name and a little bit about themselves. I knew the parents of many of them, and felt that these students all came from very good homes. How bad could they be?

This class met once a week at the school. They had a book to read about their church itself, and then how they as people were expected to behave dealing with their lives. Each week they were all expected to read a chapter and be able to tell what they read, and learned from reading it. It seemed simple enough. There were a few complaints about trying to make time for "THIS STUFF!" We tried to encourage them to at least try. We let them talk, ask questions, and voice their opinions, then ended with a prayer. They rapidly left showing me that they could not wait to get out of there!

The following week, to my shock, all the students came back. No absentees! I greeted the class, then asked how many had finished reading that chapter. Two hands were waving rapidly waiting for attention. I asked a girl in the front row what she had learned from the chapter and she did an excellent oral report. I thanked her and praised the way she explained what she had read and learned.

Julie and I had been talking during that week, and decided how hard it had to be for these kids to go to school all day, then come to this class, and talk about God. To have all the energy backed up from sitting all day and have to continues a few hours later. After some careful thought, I came up with the following plan:

Each week a different student would be chosen to read the entire chapter. The others got a break! At the next class that student was required to give a short summery of what he or she got from their homework. At that first meeting the reader gave a great talk about what she had read and how she intended to use it in her life. I thought it was an exceptional talk and told her that was exactly what we expected.

Another student was chosen for the following week.

Noticing that we still had plenty of time I told the students that I had something important to tell them. When they were all listening I began. "We understand how hard it must seem for you to go to school all day, sit in your seats and then come here. We do understand that at your age, you are full of energy and need to move around! I hope we can help you with that and still stick with the reason for this class, to help create people with a positive outlook on life, by showing them what the real world is about. We hope to make you look forward to coming here! I heard a voice, "RIGHT!" from somewhere in the back!

We got together that next week and started thinking of places we could take these students that would keep their interest and make them even better people. To our surprise our list grew rapidly. It consisted of the following and more.

1. The County Jail! We took the students there. A policeman there explained what most of the prisoners did to get there, and gave a short version of what they did daily.

2. The county Nursing Home. We took the students in groups to visit some of the patients. These people, especially the elderly, loved them. It was easy to see how grateful these residents were to talk and even laugh with their guests.

3. At Christmas time we all got together at my cabin in the woods and ate, then wrapped gifts for all the patients in the nursing home. We roasted marsh mellows outside, and sang Christmas songs. That was one our most pleasant time together.

I Never Imagined a Pen Would Change My Life

As the year went on we added other activities to our List. The students even suggested other ones. For sure they were all very interested and satisfied people! We loved our class!

We started the third week with the student who had read the chapter. She was well prepared, did an awesome job of describing what she had read, and how she had worked it into her daily life. I was proud of her and her fellow students all seem to be as well. A very short discussion took place. After that I asked the students to quietly walk out to the parking lot where I showed them which cars we were using to go on our first field trip! Afterwards, everyone was chatting on the way back to the church. It was great to hear some of the comments, and how they had enjoyed their time. My daughter and I smiled as we listened knowing we had a group of pleased and contented students.

Everyone was so well behaved. So different from what we had witnessed that first night. I personally had a special moment which went right to my heart. Mitch opened the doors for me that night. What a gentleman! Weekly that season, taking another one of our chosen trips, we had a great time with our students.

Our last get together was down to my cabin in our woods. We had a fire to roast hot dogs on, some simple drinks and snacks. The class wrapped some Christmas gifts we had gotten for people in a nursing home. Then all together we sang some Christmas carols.

When it was time to leave, Mitch got a group of his classmates to carry the gifts out to the car. Other students started picking up the used paper plates and the left over wrapping paper, and things. Wow! I was so proud of them. It brought tears to my eyes realizing that the last class was only a few weeks away. I would miss them so much.

I Never Imagined a Pen Would Change My Life

Time passed and I would often run into one of the students who stopped to talk to me. I remember a boy named Richard. He motioned for me in a store one day. "Aren't you Mrs. Fisher who had our eigth grade class?" I said," Yes, how are you doing?" He stood quiet for a minute then said. "I have to tell you that was the best class I ever had." I thanked him and we talked a bit longer then I walked away with a smile. We had made a positive made a positive difference in some very special lives.

Forward: For many years my husband and I went to a Gentleman from our church parish to have our income Taxes done. He was so kind and thorough. We enjoyed how he could do such a great job for us and still be so friendly and easy to work with. The remarkable part was he and his wife had nine children. As strange as it may seem, he always had a new story to share with us about them and it made filing our taxes something we enjoyed hearing!

Forward again: When this man stopped doing taxes we were lucky enough to have one of his sons for our accountant, and his brother, Mitch, for our Financial Advisor. I never dreamed that the young man in that eighth grade class so long ago, the one who threw his pen at me the first night, would be telling us what to do with our money, helping us make good choices. I have the highest respect for him. I totally trust him and think of him as a very close friend. I still tease him about throwing his pen at me and we both laugh.

Eight months ago, my husband Joe passed away. It is still too real for my heart to totally accept. That being said, Mitch is much more that a money advisor to me. Actually, sometimes when I have a sad day he helps me forget the financial talk for a while and he holds my hand and lets me cry. On other days, we can laugh and talk about happy things. He senses my mood and is always there to help me. Other times, when he has something little or big bothering him, I try to cheer him up. We have come a long ways since he tossed the pen at me, a long way with a very special outcome.

Getting back to the beginning of this story, with my daughters book about me and the page of those who inspired me, Mitch should be on that page as well. He is a great husband, and a wonderful father to his two children. He is a speaker at church and helps out with other things there. Everyone that I hear talk about him or his family have only good things to say about him. He knows when someone needs a friend and he knows for sure how to be one. I thank God every day for his friendship. So, Mitch, "Thank you so much for throwing the pen at me. We have come a long ways and it has been an interesting and special walk on life's path with you."

Always a friend,
Barbara Jeanne Fisher

Part 2 - Mitch's Story

Have you ever had a teacher that left an impact on you? This is the story of two teachers that did for me. The school year was 1994 through 1995, I was in the 8th grade, attending a religion class. In all the years attending this was the only year that I remember my teachers. These teachers didn't just teach from the book, they also took us out to experience life. Here are a few of those trips I remember.

I remember so well the time we went to the county jail to learn about the corrections programs and what some people had done to get arrested. We saw how the prisoners spent their days, and where they slept at night. We saw where and what they ate, exercised, and actually some of them had school classes there. It was interesting to hear how they were sometimes punished. For sure it was enough to make most of us glad we were not in there!

One evening, we went to a local nursing home. These special people, a few handicapped, many elderly were so happy to see us, visit with us and on some occasions, sing with us. It made all of us feel so happy to see how our visit had enlightened their lives and help them have a great day. Sadly, some of them never had any visitors. It made us realize how lonely their lives had to be.

At Christmas time, we all met at a cabin in the woods. While enjoying heat from a fireplace on the wall, and sharing snacks, and chatting with each other, we wrapped many gifts for the various people we had met during our classes! They were simple things to show them that someone cared about them and loved them. Later, taking them to the people also made us understand that giving to others was for sure something that fit in our CCD class. God wants all of us to care for the sick, lonely and everyone, and that is exactly what we had done! What a great feeling. I remember an additional surprise was that one of the other students was able to play the violin for us. What a great time we all had sharing music and time with our friends.

As I grew older, these events stuck with me, and in the future looking back there were religious lessons in each of these. Visiting the imprisoned, forgiving those that have wronged you, serving the time for the crime you have committed. Visiting the sick helped us remember that God is in each of us, that the poor in spirit can be lifted from talking to a nice person, and the fact we need friends in our lives who are supportive of each other to be truly happy. These are things that can be read in a book, but our teachers, Mrs. Barb Fisher and Mrs. Julie Darr took the time from their lives to show us how to experience these lessons.

The best part is, that they did this out of love. This was a voluntary position and they didn't even get paid. They must have felt the Lord reaching out to them and saying this is important and you will make time.

Our lives become more complicated as you get older; you will only do what you create time for. You will find time for what is important to you. For them, it was taking on 8th graders, the kids that are going through some of their toughest times of their lives. The body is changing, the desire to be accepted by our friends, and loved at the same time.

These teachers must have said, let's make this a priority and help these kids find their way with their faith. They must have felt this was important to make time for us kids. They even took time to take us to places so we could experience what most have only read. As I grew up, the more I appreciated that. But it was their kindness, their time, the experiences they provided is the reason why they are the only teachers I remember having with religion class.

Julie and Barbara are members of my church, and I saw them from time to time through the years. I would be nice and say hi, but that was about it. I worked several different jobs in my life, trying to find what kind of work I would enjoy. I finally came across financial advisory work.

My father was a bookkeeper, and my eldest brother is a CPA, following my father's steps. He even bought the business from Dad, which in turn took over the many clients he had established through those years.

You see, I am the 7th child of 9. In my early years of adulthood, I worked in the dental world, manufacturing custom dental prosthetics. At one time I owned a dental lab with two of my other brothers, later I worked as a salesman for a lab out of Michigan. It was during that time, I discovered my true calling as a financial advisor. I started my career with one company but ended up with another, which was in the same building as my brother's CPA firm.

One day in 2018, while working I received a call from my brother's office asking if I could meet with some clients. Of course, I said I could meet with the clients and provide some guidance. Far from my mind was the younger years of my youth. But I kept up on my faith, became married, and had children. At one point, I found out that Barb Fisher was an author and even owned a store in downtown Fremont. But I was surprised to see the clients for the meeting were Joe and Barb Fisher.

As I walked in thinking she wouldn't remember me from those many years ago, she exclaimed how she had remembered me and how I had thrown a pen at her during the first class of religion. I remembered something like that and it sounded liked something I would have done. I was surprised that a rebellious action stuck to her all these years. I admitted to her that I may have done something like that, and she informed me that I did. But she was okay with it since she needed a pen at that moment. I chuckled to myself, well at least I can teach them on some ideas for their finances. They gave me some additional information and I suggested that should we meet again, and I would have some ideas to share. Joe and Barb agreed! That pen incident wasn't as bad as I thought. Then as they got up to leave, she asked if I would ever throw another pen at her. We laughed and I said only if you need another one, and I will always have one ready for you.

I met with them to review and confirm their goals were still on track. Then one day I was informed Joe may not achieve his goal of living to the young age of 118. He continued to work on making that goal as we would meet, I would remind him of it.

One day, out of the blue Barb asked if I could have a meeting to review their stuff and they wanted to have their daughter Julie at the meeting. I agreed. I thought something was off, they never requested a meeting, and we had just recently met a few months ago for their review. Joe wanted to make sure all their stuff was with me, so it was easier to take care of. Barb was concerned that she would be on a reduced income if Joe's income was to stop. We reviewed everything and confirmed the income would be sufficient for Barb. All three, Barb, Joe and Julie seemed to be relieved, and we were on the same page. What I wasn't anticipating was the day I received the call that Joe had taken his last breath.

Barb was at a loss, not that she wasn't aware this was coming or that she couldn't handle finances. She was at loss, for she had lost the love of her life. The love these two had for each other was evident every time I met with them. The stories they shared with me on how they met, how they grew as a couple, how they would tolerate each other's uniqueness. Everything they did, they did it with love for the other. Now she has lost the love of her life, and she needed to communicate to someone about it. I was doing what I could to ease the passing of Joe. When someone passes away there is a lot of paperwork to be filled out, that's where I was helping.

One day, when I wasn't expecting, a text message came in, followed by another, and another. I believe the first time Barb texted me; it was around 7 messages. Then the next day another 8 came in. I realized how she is expressing herself, her concerns and loneliness at a time through the only format she knew best. She wrote, she is an author, and she shows it. As I arrived to work in the morning, I would anticipate messages from Barb and I would contact her to see if there was anything I can do more for her. I look forward to reading her new material, it's only for me. Can you imagine having an author to write to you exclusively? Wouldn't you treasure it as I do?

Who would have imagined that a pen incident from my youth, would ever be the start of a story about a financial advisor and an author becoming friends, who enjoy the company of each other? I can assure you; it was not me. But I am glad that it is about me, about me and Barb. Thank you, Barb, for sharing your insight on life, love, and faith with me.

About the Authors

Barbara Jeanne Fisher is also the author of two novels, Stolen Moments and Just Out of Reach. She is also well-known for her contributions to eight of the Chicken Soup of the Soul series. MS Fisher has also published two children books *How Much Can Teddy Bear* and *Nobody's Lion*. She has had hundreds of stories published in national, and international magazines including Woman's World, Guide Posts, and the Messenger of the Sacred Heart. Along with her love for writing, she also enjoys playing the piano, teaching writing classes and spending time with her friends and family.

Mitchell Holland is my most recent writing student. He naturally does what I recommend all of my students to do, *Write with your Heart*, and Only *Write About Things That You Know*. Mitch is not only a great writer, but the best friend a person could have!

WA

www.ingramcontent.com/pod-product-compliance
Lightning Source LLC
Chambersburg PA
CBHW050048080526
44586CB00014B/1510